THE DYNAMIC DUO
OF
LEAN SYSTEMS

THE POLARITY GROUP

"NEW DIRECTIONS IN MANAGEMENT"

FIVE-S SYSTEM FOR PROCESS CONTROL
&
EIGHT-D SYSTEM FOR CONTINUOUS
IMPROVEMENT AND
CORRECTIVE ACTIONS

THE DYNAMIC DUO
OF
LEAN SYSTEMS

THE POLARITY GROUP

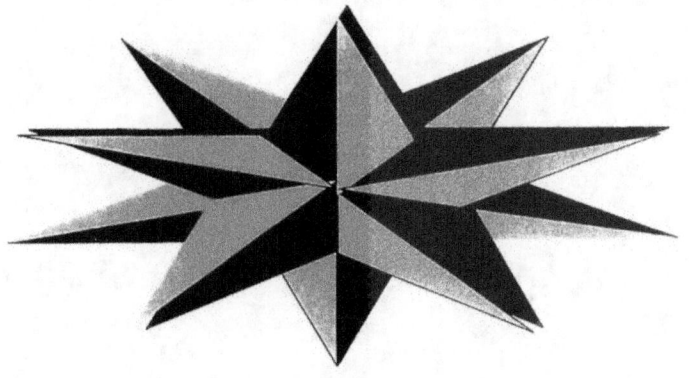

"NEW DIRECTIONS IN MANAGEMENT"

**FIVE-S SYSTEM FOR PROCESS CONTROL
&
EIGHT-D SYSTEM FOR CONTINUOUS
IMPROVEMENT & CORRECTIVE ACTION**

PART ONE

THE FIVE- S SYSTEM
FOR
PROCESS CONTROL

INTRODUCTION

It has become imperative for companies competing in today's industrial market to maintain defined, controlled, and documented manufacturing or servicing processes. Their failure to do so especially in recessionary markets will likely keep them from breaking into the coveted circle of sought after premium world market customers.

In truth, current customer demands have made process control a necessity; even without seeking certification by one or more of the internationally recognized quality standards. Organizations unable to demonstrate a solid marriage between their floor operating processes and their defined design, manufacturing, and quality systems are all too commonly seen as a bad risk by this select pool of potential customers.

The basis for this rejection by potential customers is the factor of unpredictability in delivery time, costs, and quality which are the frequent results of a shortfall in tight process control. Tight process control results in sequences being carried out in a continuum of predictability. Predictability is gained by doing things the same way each time, using the same process, same materials and the same control thereby ensuring the same result...consistency.

There are several key approaches toward these leaner manufacturing practices that can be applied today. One of these is the subject of this text and was first introduced as part of the lean manufacturing concepts as the Five–S Program. Some organizations have even up-graded this Five-S approach to a Six-S and then a Seven-S approach by adding two additional critical "S's." to the original listing.

Application of a Five, Six, or Seven-system will enhance your process control and improvement efforts to the delight and satisfaction of your company, your employees, and most of all your customers. The best part is that such a program is neither difficult nor burdensome to put into place, while the benefits derived from your efforts are almost endless.

So what is holding you back?

TABLE OF CONTENTS
PART ONE

TABLE OF CONTENTS
PART ONE (CONT.)

TABLE OF CONTENTS
PART ONE (CONT.)

SECTION ONE

THE FIVE-S SYSTEM

International quality standards along with recent economic pressures have turned industrial focus towards process control as opposed to product control. This shift in focus has highlighted some programs specified within Lean Manufacturing concepts that are designed to facilitate process control. One such approach is commonly referred to as The Five-S Program. To this concept we added what we believe to be two critical elements to the original five, thus we call our approach the Seven-S Program.

The original Five-S Program was process focused and more importantly employee oriented. The system when implemented, facilitated clear-cut control of manufacturing and service processes. The Five-S concept was first adopted by the Japanese and got its title as the five key elements of the system which were each labeled with a word beginning with an "S".

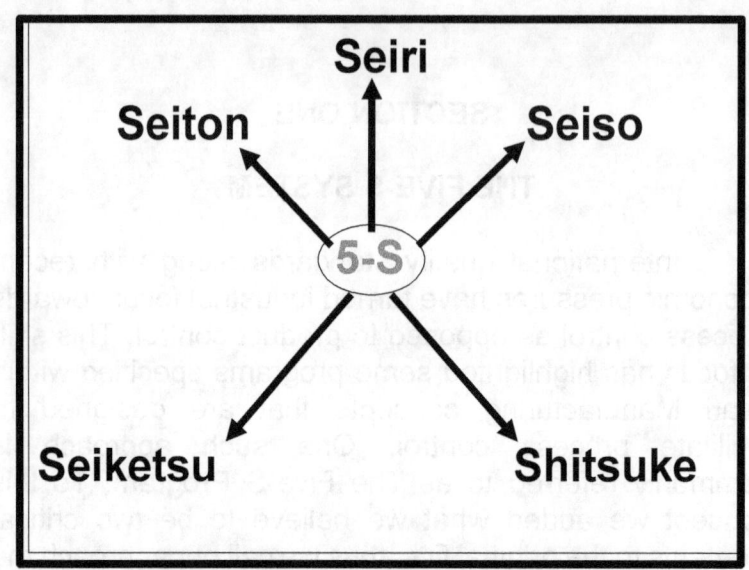

FIGURE #1 THE FIVE-S SYSTEM

The Japanese word; <u>**Seiri**</u> identifies the initial action step within the Five-S Program. This action requires the clear identification of required tools, equipment, instructions, measuring devices, floor area, etc., needed at a specific work station. Once identified these items must be separated from items which had nothing to do with the job activities or sequences to be carried out, and are therefore superfluous to the process.

The second "S"; <u>**Seiton**</u>, entails deciding on the best and most efficient location for items identified in Step One as critical to the task at hand. The appropriate placement of each needed tool or document for the process will ensure availability as the job sequences are being completed.

These first two actions, Seiri and Seiton should be carried out as a joint effort by Management, Supervisors, and the Process Operators that oversee the job sequences involved. Making this a cooperative enterprise is the total effort of all involved and will help ensure program acceptance by all participants as to where the items are located.

Seiso, the third term refers to sprucing up a work station to facilitate employee pride, which is a basic ingredient for success of this program. Employees operating specific machines or work stations are more likely to convert this pride in appearance to pride in performance; thereby helping to ensure customer satisfaction with process results.

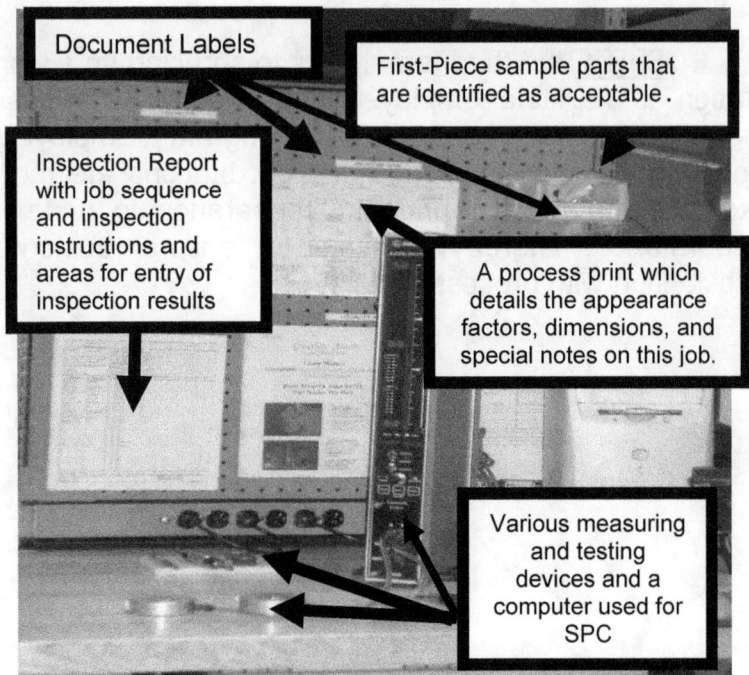

Figure # 2   A FIVE-S WORK CELL STATION

In addition to facilitating employee pride, a clean orderly work station is much more likely to result in controlled work methods and predictable results than a work station that is chaotic and uncontrolled.

The fourth Japanese term within the Five-S Program is **"Sieketsu"** meaning to practice the elements of the program on a day-to-day basis; thus making them a part of the Operator's daily work routine. The employee must be encouraged to adhere to the concepts of the program as they are established.

To be compliant with the system, each Operator must accept and learn to have only necessary items at their work station. Operators must constantly return things to their proper location when not in use, and maintain the work station in a clean manner at all times.

The fifth and last term **"Shitsuke",** encourages employees to adopt habits of compliance with the tenets of the control processes. Shitsuke requires that the entire program be monitored or audited for compliance on a regular and routine basis.

In this monitoring activity a Process Auditor will observe employees at work and report on their compliance with the requirements of the Five-S Program as well as other specified quality management or operating systems. In observing the work tasks being completed, the Auditor will note Operator work activities, the station's appearance, and quality measurements or other actions taken to ensure the processes are performed according to instructions.

It is likely that in monitoring the processes and interviewing Operators at the various work stations that your observations may result in obtaining ideas and suggestions for improving a work station or process. Those suggestions for improvement are then passed along to Management as part of the audit report so that a response may be given to the Operators involved.

In yet other instances, the observations made by the Auditor may indicate that an Operator could perform better if given additional training in certain areas such as using a gauge, or measurement device, operating a machine, etc.

SECTION TWO

IMPLEMENTING THE PROGRAM

Initially in checking into the Japanese approach for the Five-S system, many thought it to be another one of the quick fix processes that are touted and then conveniently customized to match the acceptance level of the company. Programs with only this level of commitment are generally soon abandoned or changed into something unworkable.

Others, where the Management Team is more committed, have discovered that not only did the Five-S Program make sense in theory; but it was also simple in implementation. In truth, these five elements were so non-complex and adaptable that they were almost scary.

To initiate the program and develop employee interest in the concepts involved, first gather employees assigned to work within each selected department or work cell into a training session on the concepts of the Five-S Program. During this training session it is critical for overcoming initial suspicion and criticism of the program to encourage participants to ask questions and comments as you proceed.

It is also suggested that in this familiarization training on the Five-S concepts that you inform the employees that their work station activities will be monitored to ensure compliance. This is a key part of the training and development of a solid system.

THE ORIGINAL FIVE-S CONCEPTS

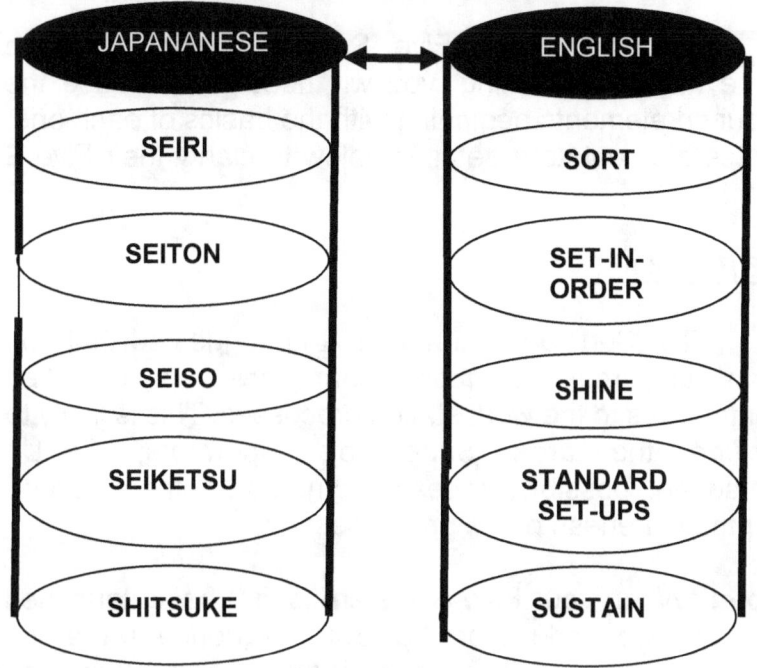

JAPANANESE	ENGLISH
SEIRI	SORT
SEITON	SET-IN-ORDER
SEISO	SHINE
SEIKETSU	STANDARD SET-UPS
SHITSUKE	SUSTAIN

FIGURE # 3 FIVE –S TERMS JAPANESE...ENGLISH

SECTION THREE
FIVE-S SYSTEM DEVELOPMENT

In setting up the Five -S Program after you have done the initial training, you will need to introduce the required elements beginning with the basics of each one. These elements are detailed below to clarify their Five-S function.

SEIRI...SORT

To "Sort" a work station, it is suggested that you form an implementation team including the key contributors to the work station processes. This is likely to include the area Supervisor; Operators; Set-Up Personnel; possibly Process Engineers or others with in-depth awareness of the processes involved.

Note: When your Five-S system is first being launched and you are working on the "Sort" sequence, it may be necessary to re-visit this activity two or three times, as individuals will tend to want to retain a few private or special "just-in-case" items.

In the process of carrying out this implementation step, it is necessary to work with all shifts or similar type processes to incorporate personal variations. This will standardize the selection of items to be sorted and retained at similar work stations and on all shifts.

To simplify the sorting activity, there are some investigative tools that can be used to facilitate the "Brainstorming" with the implementation team to gain input in breaking the process down into step by step segments. These same investigative tools will also facilitate the program's implementation as you move through the "Setting-Up" and "Standardizing" stages later.

For an initial step in the implementation process we suggest you utilize a fantastic tool that was first introduced under "Lean Manufacturing" programs being followed today.

This is a process called "Gemba" by the Japanese which facilitates team perceptions of processes being completed on the work floor.

In this activity the individual team members surround the work station and observe the work station processes in action. As the observations are being made by each team member, he/she will note everything observed while the process is being completed. This includes work sequences, work motions, walking required, safety concerns, and material storage locations. Be sure to include Lift truck involvement or people traffic in area, bending or lifting required, gauge usage measurements made, measurements recorded, etc.

This entire process may take as long as benefits can be derived. Sometimes it is even a good idea to have the team of observers change locations so that more than two eyes and ears have reviewed each process sequence from similar angles.

The notes taken from this activity do not need to be lengthy; however they should enable the facilitator to effectively participate in a team brainstorming process following the "Gemba" activity. Making sketches or taking photos of the area as the process is being completed will facilitate brainstorming observations made in completing this activity later by the implementation team

Once the process Gemba observations have been completed, the team will sit together in a quiet area or training room and brainstorm on the individual notes, sketches, or pictures they have made on the shop floor.

This brings us to the second tool to be utilized in the sorting, setting-up, and standardizing of your work stations by the Team...a "Fishbone" or Ishakawa Diagram. Using this diagram will enable your team to develop a full understanding of the criticality of each step of the process

.   In applying the fishbone diagram to your operations, you will need to explore one leg of the process diagram at a time, listing each critical or necessary item observed while doing so. As you identify those items not required in the tasks, remove them from their assigned leg of the diagram and enter a note above that leg to indicate they are not needed for the process. (A simple Fishbone diagram can be seen below).

(On each leg list those items deemed to be critical superfluous to the process.)

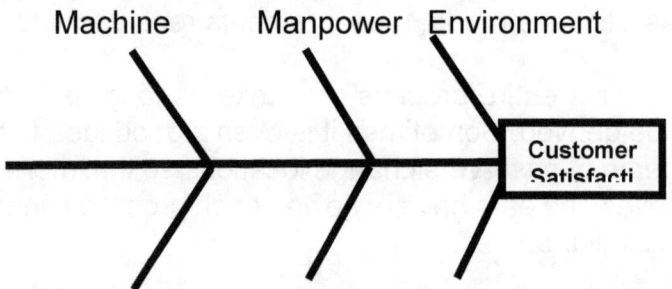

Machine   Manpower   Environment

Customer
Satisfacti

Measurement   Methods   Materials
FIGURE #4 FISHBONE DIAGRAM OF A PROCESS.

MACHINE:

In the "Machine" leg of the fishbone sketch above, your team must review the equipment or machinery required to complete the process step. Keep in mind that machinery or equipment comes in a variety of shapes, sizes, and purposes including hand tools, gauges and/or measuring devices which may be supplemental or supportive to the key process equipment utilized at this work cell or station.

Thus, in looking at key equipment such as a lathe, screw machine, or stamping press, it is also important to consider related items which are directly necessary to that unit and provide for their continued presence at the station.

METHODS:

In establishing the methods to be followed at a work station it is critical that provisions be made to identify the types of documentation and instructions required for completion.

As your team works on the methods leg of the diagram, consideration should to be given to process prints, set-up sheets or instructions, quality alerts, gauge listings, inspection instruction sheets, quality records, or preventive maintenance documents, etc. These documents need to be readily available so they may be utilized and followed whenever the process is being run, thus assuring a predictable method is being followed each time.

MATERIALS:

In setting up the work station, care should be given to allow an effective flow of materials through the work area. There will also be a need to control the flow of materials and supplies into the area. You will need to consider storage and queuing areas to allow a continued flow of materials IN, and finished products OUT.

It will also be necessary to make provisions for setting aside and final distribution of product which may be suspect or unacceptable. In this way the nonconformities are prevented from continuing through the work-flow and receiving added value or delivery
.

.MANPOWER:

As indicated earlier in the description of the Five-S implementation process, the critical human (manpower) factor is to ensure that all personnel involved in a specific work activity are trained to perform the work tasks required of them, and that they are able to operate under the Five-S Program.

This assurance can be gained in three ways:

- ✓ First, employee involved must be trained to complete the task assigned to them either through class room training or on-the-job training.

- ✓ Secondly, employee activity must be monitored to ensure that Operators are performing their assigned task as instructed, and that they are adhering to the requirements of the program.

- ✓ Third, when the program has been implemented, the monitoring is the critical portion. It is through effective and positive monitoring that employees become entrenched in applying the Five-S system.

MEASUREMENT:

As indicated above under the Sort phase of program implementation, it is expected those documents for a process will be identified as critical.

This is especially true of instructions and documentation related to verification of results located at the work station. These instructions are likely to be measurement instructions including what should be measured, using what instruments or equipment, and when such measurements are applied.

An addendum to instructional requirements is a need for a form covering retention of measurements taken in a gauging process, or in some instances, the utilization of some form of Statistical Process Control.

ENVIRONMENT:

Attention should be given to the job tasks and their related environment. Are there oven temperatures that need to be maintained or special clean environment requirements to follow? These elements must be identified up front and made part of the process picture on the Fishbone diagram for true control of the process.

When all items that have been determined to be identified as necessary or unnecessary to the process have been isolated, try a practice run through without the unneeded items. In this way your team can be assured that they are not casting aside something that might actually be needed, if special process situations arise. Omitting these items might cause an issue or slowdown of the process at some point in the future, if they are omitted.

SEITON...SET-IN-ORDER

Once the key necessary items for the process have been identified, the implementation team will need to work with the Process Operators and the Supervisors to establish the most effective placement location at the work station for each item. In some cases the item can be a few steps away from the primary work space as the process allows the Operator time to walk over and retrieve it. In others, it will be critical that the Operator be able to just reach out and grab it.

There will be differences between Operators in their individual ways of completing operational steps on different machines or shifts. Differences may be permitted if they are due to variations of right or left handed Operators, height differences etc. These variations you should consider to allow but they should be limited as much as possible.

Some companies have gone so far as to label the workbench to indicate where a specific gauge or process print might be located. Others have merely indicated a general area or location such as at one end of a machine, or on the inspection bench, or posted on the pegboard at the work bench. You may elect to specify locations for the instructional materials and documents related to the operations involved. Eventually you will be comfortable that your team has settled on the right mix, and that you are now ready to say this is the set-up needed for this job sequence.

As can be seen in the photo below there are labels on the peg board to indicate where specific items are placed.

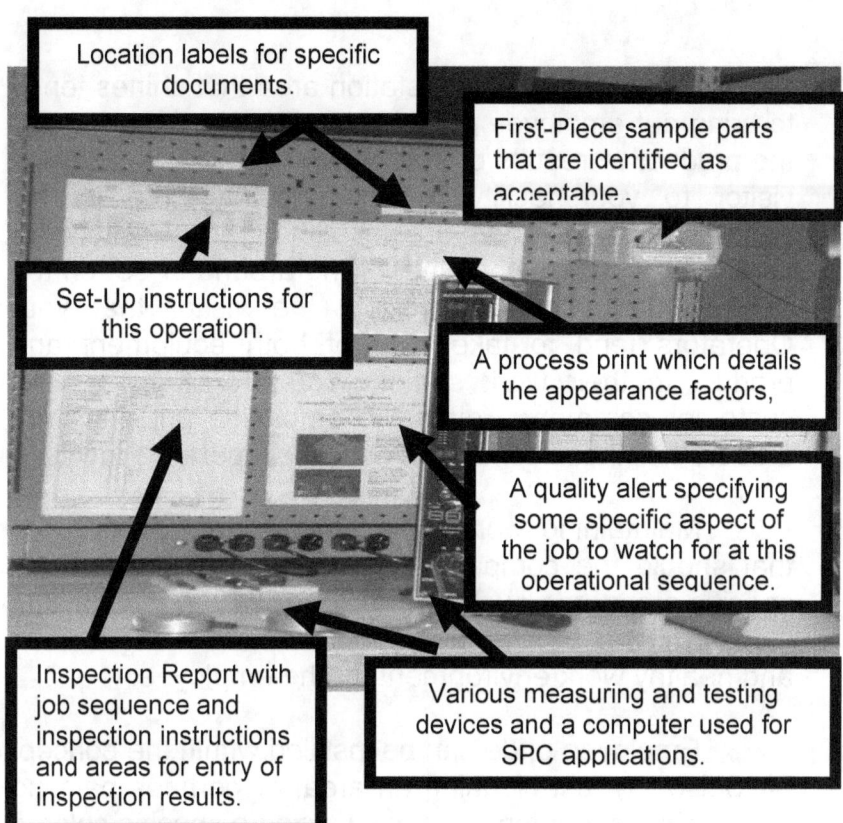

Location labels for specific documents.

First-Piece sample parts that are identified as acceptable .

Set-Up instructions for this operation.

A process print which details the appearance factors,

A quality alert specifying some specific aspect of the job to watch for at this operational sequence.

Inspection Report with job sequence and inspection instructions and areas for entry of inspection results.

Various measuring and testing devices and a computer used for SPC applications.

FIGURE # 5 WORK STATION SORTED-CLEANED AND STANDARDIZED,

SEISO...SHINE

On the surface it appears that this element of the program is strictly focused on and for the benefit of the Operator; however the primary winner in doing so is the company. To "Shine" an area is to clean it, to make it attractive so to speak. Some clients choose to paint the individual process areas and equipment a specific color to identify a type of cell or a specific department within the operations.

Some as seen in Figure #5 on the preceding page have elected to purchase new workbenches for the work stations and to set them in order for the Operator to follow. Others have simply washed or wiped down the work areas to clean.

Establishing a work station area that shines tends to bring out employee pride. This pride is translated into the productive results of that station. One of the things a visitor to your facility will immediately note is this neatness, and that there are not a lot of personal items or used coffee or pop containers lying around or set on top of machines. This signifies to the visitor that your Operators tend to take care of both equipment and product in their work station. You are likely to hear customer comments related to employee pride in their areas. Pass these comments on to the Operators involved

Maintaining work areas that shine also ensures that should the company wish to attain registration to specific standards such as the TS-16949 that a shining station will meet the requirements for maintaining a clean and healthy work environment for the employee.

Employee pride can be instilled within the concept of "Seiso" by just cleaning an area, or perhaps painting the machines, equipment, tools utilized a specific color to foster work station identity and cleanliness. Another good tool for developing employee pride is to hang signs at the work station with pictures and names of the employees who work that station; instilling in them a sense of ownership.

You can add other things to the sign such as cost of equipment, number of days without a defect, DPM's, or other statistics reflecting a positive achievement for a specific work station.

Finally, posting notices where other employees or visitors can see them to highlight cost saving ideas, or defect prevention ideas that have been developed by the team involved, will also facilitate pride within a specific work group.

SEIKETSU...STANDARDIZE

This is a key step in the Five-S implementation process. This step requires that the system be practiced and adhered to on a day-to-day basis. It is this step that demonstrates the level of employee acceptance and adherence to the program.

As part of this step in the on-going implementation work, stations are observed by all members of the team. Every time a tool, gauge, or document is out of location, it is to be immediately corrected, and the Operator re-instructed in the proper application needed when following the program.

Supervisors in these areas must make it a routine to encourage full participation of employees at all times. This should be done not through discipline, but through re-training and encouragement and with other forms of positive re-enforcement.

SHITSUKE...SUSTAIN

The fifth element of the Five-S Program "Shitsuke" entails monitoring of the entire program by an individual trained in program requirements, and who is external to the work area involved. This activity not only ensures day to day compliance within the program but also assures that your processes are being completed as specified in your operating practices.

It is the implementation and the auditing of the Five-S Program at this step that will ensure that customer requirements are met; that your processes are controlled and predictable. In the beginning of your program's implementation, this auditing may be required on a more frequent basis. Then as the program becomes routine, the auditing process may be required less frequently.

When the Auditor completes the audit of a specific department or process, a report of the findings should be given to the department Supervisor for posting in the department for employees to read and take corrective action. A copy of the report is also given to Management, as there may be areas in which Management will need to get involved. These may be areas for correction and continual improvement of the processes audited, or in scheduling some employees for additional training.

As the Auditors are monitoring the processes, here are some examples of observations that might be made:

- ✓ Where locations have been identified for critical process items at the station, are the items not in use in their proper location?

- ✓ Where there are instructions at the work station, ask the employee to indicate what part of the instructions he/she is currently completing, and to explain what must be done, how it must be done, and why?

- ✓ Where there are gauges or measurement devices at the station, verify whether or not they are in calibration.

- ✓ Have the employee demonstrate how a specific quality check is carried out with a gauge or measurement device at the station.

- ✓ What does the Operator do if the quality results are not within allowable specifications?

✓ If SPC applications are involved, (for example an X-Bar chart), have the employee complete an entry onto the chart per instructions, and then give an interpretation of what the findings indicate about the process.

✓ Where there are Preventive Maintenance actions to be carried out, is there evidence that these activities have been completed?

✓ What does the Operator like best about the process he/she is assigned to complete?

✓ What would he/she like to see changed, and why?

Note: If during the work station audit something is out of compliance, ask the Operator if he/she is aware that things are not right. If "YES", then ask why the instructions and requirements ARE not being met? It is critical that the audit process not be viewed as a "policing action", but rather as a training process. It is designed to maintain and/or improve the base processes involved.

THROUGHOUT YOUR AUDIT AND INTERVIEW WITH THE OPERATOR, ANY COMMENTS ON NONCOMPLIANCES SHOULD BE POSITIVE AND SUPPORTIVE OF THE OPERATOR AND THE FIVE-S PROGRAM AT ALL TIMES!

SECTION FOUR

EXPANDING THE PROGRAM

In this segment we introduce the two additional elements into the system bringing the total to either six or seven elements for process control. Many organizations are beginning to realize the value of these elements as factors for employee morale and cost and also for customer satisfaction.

Sixth Element...Safety:

The first of these addendums to the Five-S system is directly focused on the Manpower leg of the process fishbone diagram and is an "S" for Safety. We added the safety element because of concern for the safety of the Operators and other employees within the organization. By adding the safety element, employees can see that the company is concerned for their well-being.

It is a natural addition to the monitoring process and as far as carrying out specific job tasks, safety should be a prime concern at all times. As a part of the implementation process for the program, it is critical that employees be given training in the safety concerns at the work station.

In learning to carry out a specific work assignment, Operators are to be instructed on the need for proper utilization of personal protective devices and equipment required when performing their duties. Is hearing protection required? Safety glasses? Protective gloves, hard hat, etc.?

There should be training in how to handle an emergency shut down, or what should be done if there is a hazardous chemical spill. What guards are to be kept in place? How to complete a lockout-tag out action at the machine. In short, the existence of any hazard at the work station should be made clear to the Operator how these conditions must be handled.

When conducting the process audit at the work station, the Auditor is to ask specific questions regarding process safety. In addition, the Auditor should look for things such as the overloading of parts of products in a pan, etc., that could lead to back injury when lifted. Are skids of materials and product being stacked in a safe manner? If a lift truck is being used at the station is the truck being maintained in a safe manner, and review of the brakes, horns, lights being carried out on the truck?

By including Safety within the Seven-S program you ensure that a safe, clean, and well organized environment would be available to your employees. This Sixth-S activity in our program necessitates that all facets of safety at the work station be reviewed on an on-going basis. The work station elements for manufacturing are the same elements that function as contributors to safe work conditions and practices; thus observing and controlling elements is a natural by-product.

When implemented, this Sixth "S" for safety at one client's operation indicated that their incident rate for lost time injuries decreased to zero days without a lost time injury per one year. The improvements were credited primarily to an increase in employee safety awareness.

This safety performance improvement also had a significant positive impact on the client's Worker's Compensation costs. The injury rate for Worker's Compensation went down considerably; thereby having a positive impact on bottom line profits.

Seventh Element...Satisfaction:

The Seventh element added to a Five-S system focuses on internal and external customer Satisfaction. It is through the application of this element that the company can transfer the goals and objectives of its Management Team for customer satisfaction down to the Operators at each work station or process within the organization.

Impact from this element facilitates the awareness and concerns for customer requirements into product and service results at the work station. These demands can easily be specified as reasonable goals and objectives for the process operators in performing their day-to-day tasks.

The inclusion of this element enables the organization to incorporate a key element of ISO, and TS-16949, or other primary customer requirements into the Five–S Program. By completing the on-going audits of a work station activity, communication and pursuit of customer and organizational requirements can be traced from the top down through the organization.

THE AUDITING PROCESS

AUDIT PREPARATION

Prior to carrying out the actual audit of the work station area, the Auditor should just observe the work processes for a few minutes, noting what and how things are being done. If the work process to be audited has not been evaluated by the Auditor before, this is an excellent time to meet with the Supervisor over the process and discuss any questions the Auditor might have. Inquire of the Supervisor if there are issues or specific things that are critical to the process that should be looked at as the audit is completed.

Based upon your observations and your conversations with the departmental Supervisor, determine the critical factors of the process and prepare a checklist of questions to be pursued during the actual audit.

In completing the floor audit at a work center, begin by noting identity data such as specific machine numbers; material identities; gauge numbers; employee names; clock numbers; time of day; part numbers being processed, or other pertinent data. This information will be critical when discussing or reporting your observations to others as it will help them to understand the issues of noncompliance when reviewing the audit results.

The non-compliances and/or observations and opportunities for improvement are detailed below, and are based upon observations of work in process; Operator interviews; and review of documents and/or records relative to specific QMS; TS; ISO; and Seven-S requirements. Where there are issues to be raised, they should be clearly and concisely stated. Where possible, each issue will be supported by records or documents.

SEVEN-S
AUDIT CHECKLIST

INPUTS:	**OUTPUTS:**
Work station instructions; All applicable QMS procedures; SPC requirements; Work Process Instructions, Preventive maintenance; Inspection and measurement processes; Seven-S require- ments; Quality Alerts; Other job related aids for processing.	Observations of work area and actions; Inspection reports; inspection records; SPC records; Training recommendations; Disciplinary actions; Process corrections

| **How:** An audit of randomly selected employees will be completed at least 2 times per week. This audit is intended to secure an evaluation of their competence in performing work station operations. This evaluation will be retained by the Human Resources Manager in the employee's personal file. | **Who:** The Work Station Auditor will be responsible for selecting employees at random, and carrying out the audit process. There may also be special audits requested by Department Supervisor or other member of the firm's management group. | **Should's:** Questions based on specifica- tions for processing requirements as supplied by the customer and retained by the company. Employee may be questioned as indicated below, and must be capable of performing all aspects of the position unless the responsibility for the activity and its resultant quality is retained by another employee. |

Below are some questions to pursue when interviewing an Operator at a Work Station. Be sure to record critical information detailing the specifics of your interview.

Is the Operator aware of the goals and objectives of his/her process sequence?

Is there evidence that the employee is aware of the correct usage of instructional documents?

Does the employee understand and carry out the various identity and status tags to be used at the work station?

Does the employee understand the work station requirements within the Seven-S program?

Is he/she aware of the calibration status of all gauges and measurement devices employed in verifying the work station functions, and what to do if a gauge acceptance status is not known?

Is the employee aware of any SPC actions at his/her work station and how such actions must be completed and recorded?

Is the employee aware of how and when to use the Info-Center and the computer to obtain work instructions, and help in performing their job functions?

Is the Operator aware of Personal Protective Devices required at the station, and is he/she using them appropriately?

Does the employee know of safety hazards related to the processes being completed?

Have the employee demonstrate to you how a specific process instruction or measurement process is carried out, and explain to you, where in the instructive documents these instructions for doing so are located?

The foregoing listing of questions that would yield indicators of noncompliance with Five-S requirements is best put into some standard format. A standard form will enable the Systems Administrator to effectively make comparisons as to the program's effectiveness over extended periods of time. The form's make up for conducting internal audits is best designed by the Administrator as the application of the form will require additional auditors to be trained, depending on the size of the company.

As audits are conducted, by reviewing areas of noncompliance or shortfalls. The Administrator will be able to see trends which might indicate areas of potential system failure; then make corrections to keep the Five-S system on track.

Over the following pages, we will offer a sample audit form that has been applied in some organizations to monitor their Five-S Systems. The form is first presented in breakouts of the sections to be covered.

. The breakout of sections of the form are intended to clarify the system applications and practices on the shop floor in relation to the Five-S Program.. It is also intended that the breakdown in the audit form questions can double as a training tool for training additional auditors to help support the system.

Feel free to make modifications to the form presented so that it will dovetail into your organization as tightly as possible. Or if you prefer design, your company's own audit form for your Five-S Program. You are however, cautioned that developing and following some format as an audit form will be critical to your program's success as it facilitates consistent surveillance of performance.

Beginning at the top of the first page of the Five-S Audit Form is a section in which the Auditor will insert the primary identity data relating to the work station, the job or task to be completed, and the individual Operator assigned to complete the Task.

Gathering the identity information called for above the first row of check boxes is critical. It will be needed later for any discussion of observations that have been made, whether those observations are positive or negative, (This is also a section of the form that you are going to need to modify so that the identity questions will match your organization's structure.)

SAMPLE FIVE-S AUDIT FORM

Auditor: Date: Time: Operator I.D.

Department;   Work Center: Operation/part#

Section One: System Compliance:

SORT   SET/ORDER   SHINE.....STANDARDIZE.....SUSTAIN

☐   ☐   ☐   ☐   ☐

SAFETY   SATISFACTION

☐   ☐

If an element is noncompliant place "NC" in the corresponding box. If possible take photos, make sketches, or special notes

Gathering the identity information called for outside the initial box can be obtained very easily as you first meet with the Operator at the work cell or as you pursue other questions during the audit. In most cases you will not need to ask direct questions to obtain the ID information as most of it will be found on documents which you will be reviewing during your audit.

In Section One of the form you will be making an evaluation as to whether or not the Station is in compliance with Five-S requirements. As initial observations are made of the work cell, it can readily be seen if items are in appropriate places, posted neatly, and if the area is clean, organized, and polished.

Based upon these observations an entry should be made in the box under the item. If it appears that the item is not in compliance, put "NC" in the box. If it appears to be in compliance, place "C" in the box. As you pursue the audit you will be able to verify your initial observations, or if necessary, adjust them in your report summary.

It is suggested that for any item you are marking as "NC", that you take photos or make notes as to what led to your evaluation. You will need these for your report.

Exploring the elements of Safety and Satisfaction can best be done during your audit enquiries by asking the questions indicated in the question boxes on the audit form for Safety and Satisfaction.

As you did for the first items through Standardize, you should also place a "C" or "NC" into the boxes for Safety or Satisfaction.

Again, if you're rating the item as "NC", it is critical to have notes or photos to support your findings when they are being discussed after your audit.

As for the Five-S element "Sustain" this will be reviewed as you pursue the rest of the audit and are making your observations. Look for forms used to record data related to the process they should be completed in all detail. If the forms appear to be haphazard in data collection, this would indicate the compliance is not sustained and should be noted in your report.

If items or documents are not in their appropriate location it could be a lack of sustained compliance. If gauges are found to be out of calibration, again this could be a sign of an unsustained work station.

In pursuing compliance levels by using the questionnaire, it is important to remember that the questions listed are just "surface" questions. Depending upon how the Operator answers each one should be a trigger for the Auditor. If it appears that the Operator is knowledgeable and can demonstrate what he/she is saying, then additional inquiry is not likely to reveal more.

If on the other hand, the answer appears to be vague or unsure, then it might be well served to follow up with additional inquiries in this area of the system until definitive status can be reached.

Section Two...Document Awareness

The documents at a work station generally include set-up instruction sheets; inspection instructions indicating methods; points of inspection, and specifications for results. Inspection records for recording the results; product prints; preventive maintenance records; quality alerts, or other documents used by the organization may also be present.

The documents within your organization will likely be somewhat different. Therefore it will be necessary to modify the questions in this section to meet the requirements of your company.

Following each question are letter groupings; "C" ; "NC"; and "NP". If you believe the Operator's actions are compliant Circle "C". If not compliant, circle "NC".

The "NP" is to be circled if during the audit you did not directly pursue the question in which case you were not able to evaluate the status.

In completing an audit of documents and other segments in relation to the questions on the form, many can be answered by observation and do not require that the question be asked, For example: If tooling. Documents, or gauges are not in proper location this is likely to be obvious.

SECTION TWO: DOCUMENT AWARENESS
Are all required documents posted? C NC NP

Are documents posted at proper locations? C NC NP

Is the Operator able to explain the use of the documents?
  C NC NP

Can the Operator explain callouts on prints? C NC NP

Can the Operator show how to measure a specific callout?
  C NC NP

Can the Operator explain application of Quality Alerts?
  C NC NP

If an Operator is measuring something instead of asking about the document; rather ask the Operator to show you how he knows to make that measurement. This will lead you to know if he/she is aware of documents such as prints, or inspection instructions or how to record the results. Observing an action can usually provide more information than a direct question. Direct questions can clarify; observations raise questions.

Section Three: Measurement Awareness

In this segment of questions, you are seeking to attain some idea as to the effectiveness with which the Operator is capable of measurement or verification of process results. Based upon these questions, the Auditor will determine whether or not the topic should be pursued to a greater depth.

SECTION THREE: MEASUREMENT AWARENESS:

Have the Operator verify calibration of gauges at station.
    C NC NP

Have the Operator select proper gauge for a specific dimension.   C NC NP

Have the Operator perform the measurement with the gauge.   C NC NP

If If there is a rejected part at the station have the Operator check the part and tell you why it was rejected.
        > C NC NP

Have the Operator enter inspection results on the inspection record form. C NC NP

Section Four: Special Related Processes.

When responses to any of the questions in Section Four indicate that the Operator must complete a special action, you should have the Operator demonstrate how that action is completed. Be sure to look at measurements, and recording of results from the special process for a complete understanding.

SECTION FOUR: SPECIAL RELATED PROCESSES:

Can the Operator complete SPC actions? C NC   NP

Can the Operator use special devices, such as computers, comparators, profilometers; as required? C NC   NP

If required can the Operator Prepare Heat Treat Samples?
      C NC NP
If required can Operator complete Magnaflux Testing?
C   NC NP

Section Five: Safety Issues:

Sections Five and Six will only be applicable if the organization decides to expand the Five-S Program to include the additional sections on Safety and Satisfaction.

In making this decision companies can position the system to provide two powerful benefits with very little additional investment of any type. The first benefit is a reduction in cost resulting from industrial accidents of all types.

SECTION FIVE: SAFETY:

Is the Operator familiar with Lockout-Tag-Out Rules? C NC...NP

Does the Operator know where emergency shut offs are for the equipment> C NC NP

Is the Operator using required Personal Protective Equipment? C NC NP

Are Machine Guards in Place? C NC NP

A second benefit or gain is achieved by adding Safety. Do so sends a signal to the employees that the company is not only concerned about bottom line improvements that save money, but that they are also deeply concerned for the safety and well-being of its employees through continuous improvement in Safety on the job as well.

Section Six: Satisfaction:

This section is aimed at satisfying both internal and external customers of a process's product or services, leading to overall customer satisfaction.

It is critical that employees are aware of what the company's external customers are expecting or demanding, and the impact of those expectations on their process. What are the critical customer requirements?

On an internal basis, the Operator needs to understand why the product or service they are producing and sending on to the next value added operation must meet specifications in all areas. This enables the next work process to be completed in a manner that will enable them to perform to expectations as well.

Finally the Upper Management Team of the organization establishes specific goals and objectives that must be attained during a fiscal year or other period. It is critical that each Operator be aware of how these goals and objectives impact his/her operations. The questions in this section are intended to identify the Operator's awareness of what must be done to assist the company in meeting goals and expectations.

```
SECTION SIX: SATISFATION:

Does the Operator know the company's Quality
Statement?
        C  NC  NP

Does the Operator know the Objectives and goals for
various levels of the company, especially in his/her area?
        C  NC  NP

Is the Operator aware what requirements in his/her
process are critical to the Customer?  C  NC  NP
```

Section Seven: Feedback Questions:

The intention of this segment is to provide an opening for the Operator to insert some ideas or questions to the Auditor on his/her feelings about the task, equipment, or requirements on the job,

```
SECTION SEVEN: FEEDBACK QUESTIONS:

What does the Operator like best about the tasks
involved?
        C  NC  NP

What would the Operator like to have changed?
        C  NC  NP

How Long has the Operator been performing on this
task?
        C  NC  NP
```

FIVE-S AUDIT FORM

Auditor: Date: Time: Operator I..Dept.

Section One: System Compliance:

SORT   SET/ORDE   SHINE .STANDARDIZE....SUSTAIN

☐   ☐   ☐   ☐   ☐

SAFETY   SATISFACTION

☐   ☐

if element is noncompliant, place "NC" in the
corresponding box. If possible take photos, make
sketches, or special notes

SECTION ONE: DOCUMENT AWARENESS

Are all documents posted as required? C   NC   NP

Are documents posted at proper location? C NC   NP

Is the Operator able to explain the use of the
documents?
   C NC   NP

Can the Operator explain callouts on the prints?
 C NC   NP

Can the Operator show how to measure a specific
callout?
   C NC NP

Can the Operator explain application of Quality
Alerts?
 C NC NP

Can Operator explain preventive maintenance
needs?

FIVE-S AUDIT FORM (SIDE ONE CONT.)

SECTION TWO: DOCUMENT AWARENESS

Are all documents posted as required? C NC NP

Are documents posted at proper location? C NC NP

Is the Operator able to explain the use of the documents?
  C NC NP

Can the Operator explain callouts on the prints? C NC NP

Can the Operator show how to measure a specific callout?
  C NC NP

Can the Operator explain application of Quality Alerts?
  C NC NP

Can Operator explain preventive maintenance needs?
  C NC NP

SECTION THREE: MEASUREMENT APPLICATIONS:

Have the Operator verify calibration of gauges at station.
  C NC NP
Have the Operator select proper gauge for a specific dimension.
  C NC NP

Have the Operator perform the measurement with the gauge.
  C NC NP

If If there is a rejected part at the station, have the Operator check the part and tell you why it was rejected.> C NC NP

Has the Operator entered inspection results on the inspection record form? C NC NP

SECTION FOUR: SPECIAL RELATED PROCESSES:

Can the Operator complete SPC actions? C NC   NP

Can the Operator use special devices, such as computers, comparators, Profilometers; as required? C NC   NP

If required can the Operator Prepare Heat Treat Samples?
        C NC NP
If required can Operator complete Magnaflux Testing?
C NC   NP

SECTION FIVE: SAFETY:

Is the Operator familiar with Lockout-Tag-Out Rules?
        C NC...NP

Does the Operator know where emergency shut offs are for the equipment? C NC NP

Is the Operator using required Personal Protective Equipment? C NC   NP

SECTION SIX: SATISFATION:

Does the Operator know the company's Quality Statement?
        C NC   NP

Does the Operator know the Objectives and goals for various levels of the company, especially his/her area?
        C NC   NP

Is the Operator aware what requirements in his/her process are critical to the Customer? C NC NP

Can the Operator explain what must be done in the process to meet the customer's requirements? C NC   NP

SAMPLE OF A WRITTEN REPORT ON AN INTERNAL AUDIT OF A CLIENT'S SEVEN-S PROGRAM AT ONE WORK STATION

OBSERVATIONS:

Looked at several work stations in CNC to determine gage compliance and found one Micrometer that was beyond calibration date. Gage was being used by Mario working at a Star work cell.

I took the Micrometer to the gage lab and had it calibrated and returned it to Mario. The gage had been due for calibration since 07/25/15 almost a month before.

Because of the gage issue I decided to target Mario's operations for the in-depth audit.

When I returned to carry out the audit, I had Luis with me to interpret; however Mario said he could handle the English okay.

The first thing I looked at was the IR (Inspection Report) for a machine running P/N 212156; Job number 05124-001-PPAP. The job was apparently started and given first piece approval on 7/31/15. It had data entered from running on 8/1 and 8/4/15.

It was running today 08/13/15, I asked Mario if he ran the job yesterday, he said, "Yes, and Monday also". He also said the job was being run at night. According to the IR record there has been no verification of parts as required by the IR sheet on either shift since 8/8/15.

When requested to do so, he showed me how to perform the inspection processes and said he had been doing them. He just did not bother to mark them down on the IR.

Mario was also operating a second Star machine on which he was running P/N 603347-00 for job # 05019-004-SR-08SR. The same was true for this Machine. There were no inspection verification records entered for either first or second shift.

I told Mario that he was required to complete the IR sheet as we need to have the verification data for the job. I told him that if this condition occurred again he would be written up for not following the procedure.

This condition constitutes a Major non-compliance. We will need to monitor and correct the second shift Operators as well

I reviewed inspection reports at four other work stations with other Operators and they were being filled in correctly. Next week when I am in, I will have a demonstration of inspection procedures carried out at each machine to determine the level of compliance and competence.

I have attached copies of the Inspection reports to the original audit report retained in the Management Representative's Office.
External Seven-S Auditor.08/13/15

SECTION FIVE

MAINTAINING YOUR SYSTEM

SYSTEM ADMINISTRATOR REVIEWS

It is critical to the success of your Five-S, Six-S, or Seven-S Program that the System Administrator assigned be someone who believes in the value of such a system. It is important that he/she be given ample time to administrate and continually drive and follow through on all aspects of the system.

In addition to developing the procedures needed to implement your system, the System Administrator selected will need to conduct training of those procedures. This training should be given to each level of the organization. This depth of training will be necessary to attain a high degree of buy-in of all aspects of the program. Commitment and Acceptance at all levels is critical for a Program's success!

The best way to do this is to follow up on every phase of your program with the appropriate personnel until any issue that arises is resolved.

OPERATOR FEEDBACK:

This is especially critical in situations that are related to the Operator of a work station and the processes involved. If the issue is a matter of non-compliance, then make sure that appropriate training or other follow through takes place immediately.

If the issue is an employee suggestion for some sort of change in the station, set-up, or process, respond to it as quickly as you can; whether that response is positive or negative.. In addition, depending on the content of the suggestion, make sure that any impact on other Operators or work station is clearly communicated.

Whenever possible, acknowledge employees who are compliant with the program and give as much positive feedback from your auditing observations as you can.

MANAGEMENT REVIEW:

When you are establishing your Five-S system, be sure to develop some form of system reporting to your Management group. This reporting should include baseline measurements to indicate the effectiveness of existing production and quality. As your system evolves, you should be able to demonstrate gains made as a return on investment of capital and time utilized by the Five-S system. This is necessary to continue justification and acceptance of the program.

<u>NEED HELP?</u>

<u>HAVE QUESTIONS OR COMMENTS?</u>

Contact the Author: George "Bill" Browning at:

The Polarity Group
603 Nordic Ct.
Libertyville, IL. 60048
(847) 362-7152

Polaritygroup@aol.com

PART TWO

THE 8-D PROBLEM SOLVING & CONTINUOUS IMPROVEMENT PROCESS

47

TABLE OF CONTENTS
PART TWO

INTRODUCTION

SOME INTIAL CAUTIONS
ERROR NUMBER ONE-OVERUSE
ERROR NUMBER TWO-
SHORTCUTTING
ERROR NUMBER THREE-LACK OF
TRAINING

SECTION ONE
GETTING STARTED-PREPARATIONS

FIGURE #1 BLOCK DIAGRAM OF 8-D STEPS

STEP ONE-PREPARATIONS'

FIGURE #2 LEVELS OF 8-D PREPARATIONS

FIGURE #3 POSSIBLE INFORMATION GATHERING QUESTIONS

ESTABLISHING A PROBLEM SOLVING TEAM

FIGURE #4 TEAM MEMBER REQUIREMENTS
TEAM RECORDER
TEAM CHAMPION

SECTION TWO
DESCRIBING THE PROBLEM

STEP TWO-DESCRIBING THE PROBLEM

TABLE OF CONTENTS
PART TWO (CONTINUED)

FIGURE #5 SOME POTENTIAL ITEMS TO BE CONSIDERED IN PROBLEM IDENTIFICATION

<u>SECTION THREE</u>
INTERIM CONTAINMENT ACTIONS

STEP THREE: PLUGGING THE GAPS-INTERIM ACTIONS

FIGURE # 6 INTERIM CONTAINMENT ACTIONS

<u>SECTION FOUR</u>
ANALZING THE PROBLEM

STEP FOUR ANALYZING THE PROBLEM

IDENTIFY AND VERIFY THE ROOT CAUSE

FIGURE # 7 5W2H DIAGRAM

WHAT QUESTIONS
WHY QUESTIONS
WHERE QUESTIONS
WHEN QUESTIONS
WHO QUESTIONS
HOW MUCH (QUANTITY) QUESTIONS
HOW OFTEN (FREQUENCY) QUESTIONS)
IDENTIFY CRITICAL ISSUES

TABLE OF CONTENTS
PART TWO (CONTINUED)

SECTION FIVE
CONVERTING THE ANALYSIS INTO AN ACTION PLAN

STEP FIVE: IDENTIFY POSSIBLE SOUTINS

TABLE OF CONTENTS
PART TWO (CONTINUED)

FIGURE #13 IDENTIFYING SOLUTIONS
TABLE OF CONTENTS
PART TWO (CONTINUED)

SECTION SIX
VALIDATING CORRECTIVE/CONTINUOUS IMPROVEMENT PLANS

STEP SIX: VALIDATING THE CORRECTIVE ACTIONS TAKEN

FIGURE # 14 SOLUTION VALIDATION DIAGRAM

SECTION SEVEN
PREVENTION APPROACHES

STEP SEVEN: PREVENTING RECURRENCES OF ROOT CAUSE

FIGURE #15 RECURRENCES OF ISSUES AND EXPANDING APPLCATIONS DIAGRAM

FIGURE #16 DIAGRAM OF POSSIBLE SOURCES TO IDENTIFY EXPANDED APPLICATION

TABLE OF CONTENTS
PART TWO (CONTINUED)

INTRODUCTION

The material you are about to review is based upon the Eight-D Problem-Solving approach originated by Ford Motor Company, and since then passed along to the supplier base that serviced them. Since that time it has ceased being a proprietary system and has been adopted by many companies throughout the world; expanding rapidly because of its effectiveness in resolving critical issues.

In many applications, variations of the basic eight steps within the system have been introduced; however, few of these adaptations have altered the core elements of the original program. This adherence to the basic principles has continued as strict application of the key elements has led to successful resolution of critical issues. The primary reason for the system's endurance is the success of the program's attainment of customer satisfaction with a company's corrective actions when problems have been encountered.

In addition to using the concepts of 8-D for problem solving, it is our contention that the same approach can be applied to facilitate continuous improvement projects within your operation. Thus, when you see the terms "Problem Solving" or "Corrective Action", you may substitute the term "Continuous Improvement", as the activity is applicable in all cases.

Under the umbrella of a Lean Manufacturing, the principles and concepts of the 8-D process with the inclusion of the "Gemba" approach introduced by the Japanese, makes a solid addition to the corrective action and continuous improvement system

Now on with the show!

SOME INITIAL CAUTIONS

There are three common types of errors committed by some companies as they initiate their implementation of an 8-D Program These errors leading to almost certain failure are discussed at the very start of the program, as we believe that an immediate awareness of each is the best way to protect against their occurrence within your program.

ERROR NUMBER ONE--OVERUSE:

Organizations implementing an 8-D process frequently encounter some initial success just from the old Hawthorne Effect (The impact gained by giving something sudden and strong attention where previously, there had been little or no attention given at all.) Because of these initial gains, the company begins to apply the concept to an increasing number of issues; hoping to fix everything by applying the Eight-D approach.

A new system if overused will quickly become overloaded, thus undermining its potential for continued success. When overused, the 8-D approach can become burdensome, time consuming, costly, and will collapse of its own weight.

ERROR NUMBER TWO--SHORTCUTTING:

Shortcutting is a second common error; especially in those companies that fall victim to error Number One (Overuse). Taking shortcuts when carrying out any of the eight steps will eventually erode the processes and endanger the continued success of the program:

Shortcutting can lead to a hasty development of a problem statement, misdirect efforts, and lead to an inaccurate statement.
Shortcutting can lead to failure of the teams to accurately and completely identify the root cause(s) of the problem.

Shortcutting can lead to failure of the teams to identify all possible resolutions to the problems.

Shortcutting can lead to failure of the teams to implement the best approach for long-term resolutions to problems.

Shortcutting can lead to failure of the team to prevent the same or similar problems from recurring in the future.

ERROR NUMBER THREE--LACK OF TRAINING:

A third reason for program failure is a lack of team training. The 8-D system is a planned approach incorporating some specific methods for completing each step of the process.

It is critical that each individual participating on a problem solving team, whether as an active member or as a supporting player, be trained in the application of the 8-D process steps.

A complete understanding of the processes involved is needed to facilitate a cooperative effort between team members and external individuals who might be encountered in the resolution efforts, or in supporting the program in some other manner. Thus, complete acceptance of the concept is required.

The training, though required, is simple and easy for all potential team members and supporting personnel to assimilate. In this text you will be given a complete guideline for training your employees and implementing the 8-D approach for problem resolution within your facility.

SECTION ONE

GETTING STARTED...PREPARATIONS!

We begin our process journey with a quick overview of each of the eight activities involved, starting with the first step, PREPARATIONS. These steps are pictured in the block diagram shown below.

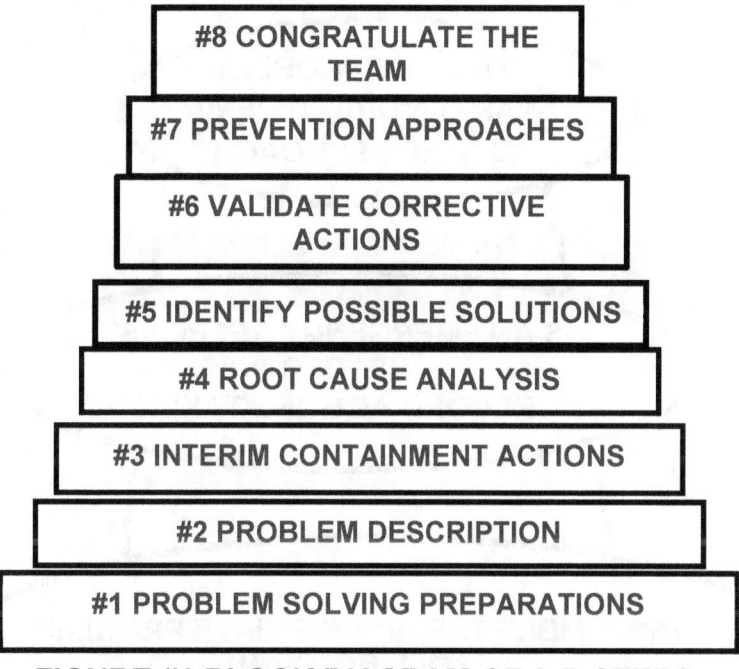

FIGURE #1 BLOCK DIAGRAM OF 8-D STEPS.

STEP ONE-PREPARATIONS:

Proper preparation is a key part of successful problem resolution. There are three actions involved in this preparatory phase. The first step in implementing a problem solving program such as the 8-D method is critical, and great care needs to be given in the selection of an issue and preparatory actions involved.

57

PREPARATION

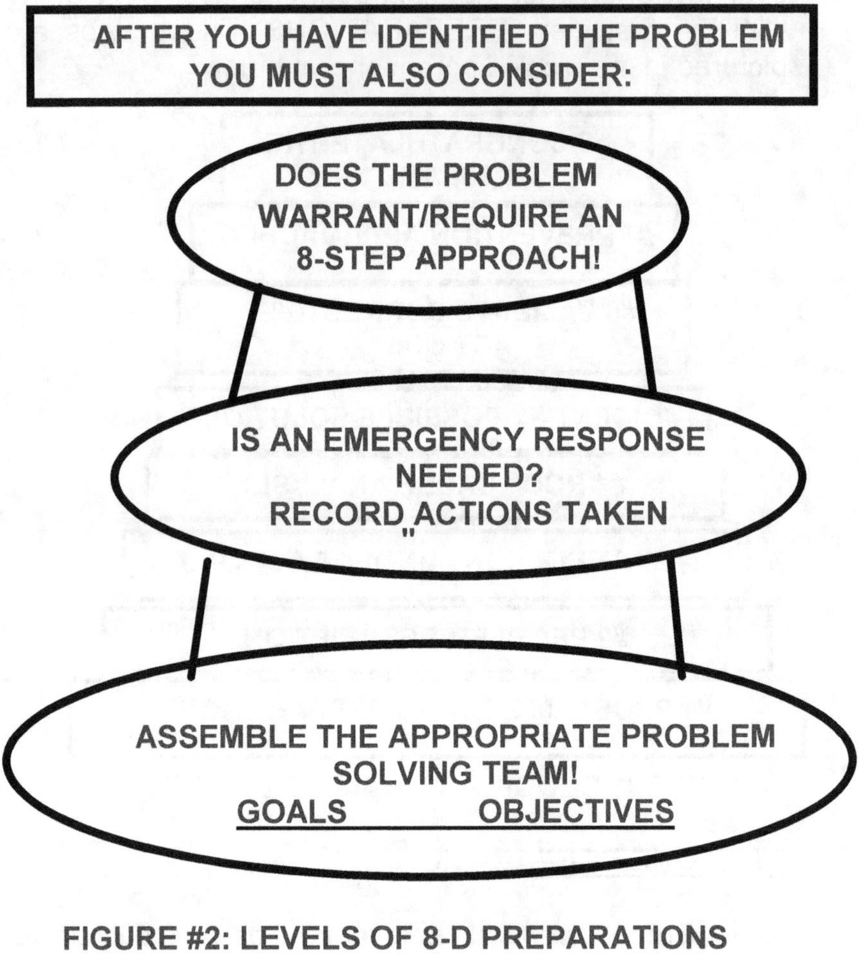

AFTER YOU HAVE IDENTIFIED THE PROBLEM
YOU MUST ALSO CONSIDER:

DOES THE PROBLEM
WARRANT/REQUIRE AN
8-STEP APPROACH!

IS AN EMERGENCY RESPONSE
NEEDED?
RECORD ACTIONS TAKEN

ASSEMBLE THE APPROPRIATE PROBLEM
SOLVING TEAM!
GOALS   OBJECTIVES

FIGURE #2: LEVELS OF 8-D PREPARATIONS

Proper actions during the preparation approach will not only succeed in correcting an organization's nastier problems and prevent their recurrence; but it will also prevent the system from becoming overburdened.

Issues that are not complex, which can be handled by one or two individuals are better off remaining outside the 8-D process. Generally, a company should establish and follow guidelines to determine which problems are to be submitted for 8-D resolution.

These guidelines may be based upon internal organizational factors such as the monetary impact given to an issue, or other negative impacts such as customer satisfaction, employee safety, or similar key issues confronting the organization. In order to effectively make meaningful problem selections and to assign an appropriate problem solving team to work on the issue, basic information gathering is critical.

Initially, the information gathered is superficial as it is targeted only on leading to some basic decisions. Questions which might be asked to assist in your go-ahead decision are suggested below.

1. Does the issue fall within the company guidelines to warrant acceptance into the 8-D process?

2. Is there immediate action required to contain additional loss to the company through incurring more value added to unacceptable product or service or by creating additional customer dissatisfaction? A listing of possible inquiries to be made to gather this preliminary information is shown on the next page.

WHAT PROCESS ACTIONS WERE BEING CARRIED OUT WHEN THE PROBLEM OCCURRED?

WHERE WAS THE ISSUE FIRST DISCOVERED AND BY WHOM?

HOW MANY UNITS WERE INVOLVED, ACTUALLY AND POTENTIALLY?

WHAT SPECIFIC PIECE OF EQUIPMENT WAS BEING USED?

DID THE ISSUE COME TO LIGHT THROUGH INTERNAL OR EXTERNAL NOTIFICATION?

HAVE ALL INSPECTION AND QUALITY RECORDS BEEN GATHERED?

WHAT PROCESS DOCUMENTS AND INSTRUCTIONS RELATED TO THIS ACTIVITY WERE AVAILABLE AT THE TIME OF OCCURRENCE?

WHAT IS THE PRIOR RUN HISTORY OF THIS OR RELATED PARTS OR SERVICE?

HAVE THE PERSONNEL INVOLVED BEEN FULLY TRAINED IN CORRECT PROCEDURES APPLIED IN THIS 8D PROCESS?

ADD ANY OTHER QUESTIONS THAT MIGHT BE MORE APPROPRIATELY ASKED WITHIN YOUR ORGANIZATION.

FIGURE #3 POSSIBLE INFORMATION GATHERING QUESTIONS.

-ESTABLISHING A PROBLEM SOLVING TEAM

Assuming that the preliminary information gathered on an issue indicates that the issue is within the guidelines for acceptability under the 8-D program, it will then be necessary to determine who should be members of the problem resolution team.

Selection of the appropriate team members is critical to the success of your problem solving effort and must be carefully completed by the Team Leader. The individuals selected by the Team Leader should be familiar with the work areas, equipment, and processes used for the manufacturing or service sequences in which the problem was created. In Addition, individuals selected should have the following attributes to be effective participants and contributors to the process.

BE TRAINED IN THE PROCESSES OF THE 8-D PROBLEM SOLVING APPROACH.

BE A SMALL SELECT GROUP OF FROM 3-TO 8 MEMBERS.

HAVE THE SKILLS AND KNOWLEDGE OF THE PROCESS IN WHICH THE ISSUE IS CENTERED.

BE ALLOWED THE APPROPRIATE TIME AND AUTHORITY TO INVESTIGATE AND RESOLVE THE ISSUE.

FIGURE #4 TEAM MEMBER REQUIREMENTS

As the Team is being assembled, the Team Leader will need to assign some basic responsibilities within the Team Members.

TEAM RECORDER:

This individual will be responsible for maintaining notes and summaries of team meetings, discussions, and all activities carried out by the Team in its resolution efforts.

TEAM CHAMPION:

This should be an individual who has a significant interest in getting the issue resolved and will therefore push others to keep the resolution process moving in a positive manner. Preferably, the person selected should be a member of Management who will be in a position to demand the cooperation of others within the organization to implement the various action steps required for issue resolution.

In addition, making each of the other Team members responsible for some aspect of the Team's activities tends to maintain focus and enthusiasm for the resolution process.

SECTION TWO

DESCRIBING THE PROBLEM

STEP TWO--DESCRIBING THE PROBLEM:

When the Team Leader is given a problem to be resolved, there should be a clear message from Management as to the scope of the problem including goals, objectives, timing, cost limitation's and other parameters defining the boundaries of the resolution process.

The Team Leader will present Management's scope statement for the process and basic information known on the issue at the Team's initial meeting. Based upon this information the Team will develop a problem statement for their resolution process.

It is critical in developing a problem statement that all information gathered be considered. The figure #5 on the next page shows a diagram of some potential items to be considered.

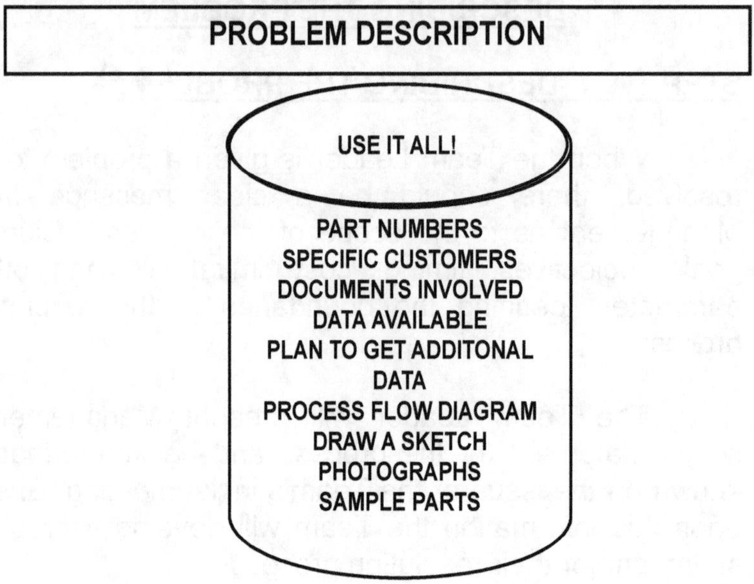

```
┌─────────────────────────────────────────────┐
│            PROBLEM DESCRIPTION                │
└─────────────────────────────────────────────┘
```

USE IT ALL!

PART NUMBERS
SPECIFIC CUSTOMERS
DOCUMENTS INVOLVED
DATA AVAILABLE
PLAN TO GET ADDITONAL
DATA
PROCESS FLOW DIAGRAM
DRAW A SKETCH
PHOTOGRAPHS
SAMPLE PARTS

**FIGURE #5 SOME POTENTIAL ITEMS TO BE
CONSIDERED IN PROBLEM IDENTIFICATION.**

The Team is to develop a clear and concise statement of the problem including the objectives to be attained in resolving the issues.

The most common error in developing a problem statement is to specify only symptoms rather than a root cause possibility. When this is done, the resolution process is likely to correct symptoms but not address the root cause that created the issue in the first place...thus the true problem is very likely to happen again.

With an accurate, complete, clear, and concise problem statement, the Team is ready to work on resolution of the defined issues..

SECTION THREE

PLUG THE GAPS...INTERIM ACTIONS

While the Team has been developing a problem statement, a couple of the members should be ascertaining the extent of the problem by determining other products and/or services that might have been impacted by this issue. The extent of impact study is a key part of the process, and is needed to prevent additional value from being added by continuing to work on product that might also be defective with the same issue.

In this phase, a decision must be made immediately upon discovery of expanded issue impact as to whether or not some type of emergency or temporary action needs to be taken to stop any further damage from the issue.

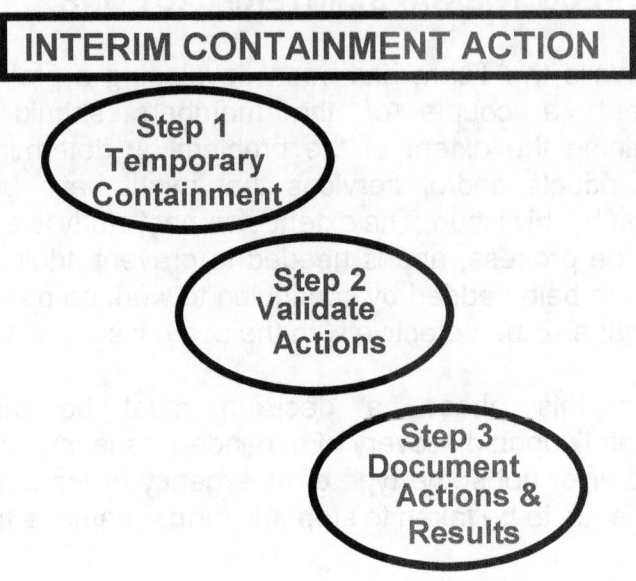

INTERIM CONTAINMENT ACTION

Step 1
Temporary
Containment

Step 2
Validate
Actions

Step 3
Document
Actions &
Results

FIGURE #6 EMERGENCY INTERIM ACTIONS

STEP THREE...INTERIM ACTIONS

Possible temporary actions include immediate contact with the Customer to assure them that the issue is being addressed, and to see if there is something that your organization can do to ease any hardships you may have created for that Customer. Give the Customer information as to emergency actions you are taking to stop the flow of deviant products, ensuring that no additional rejects will be sent to them.

If additional questionable products are on route for delivery, tell the Customer whether these products are likely to be contaminated or not.

You will also need to inform them as to when you will be getting back with additional information about the issue. Other emergency actions may be required within your own operations to determine if there are other products in process that might have the same issues. If so, immediately remove such product from the operational process flow until appropriate required containment actions can be completed such as sorting and repair.

As problems are likely to take some time to develop and implement corrective actions for eliminating the root causes of a problem; it is absolutely critical to prevent a repeat incident while the deliberation on the issue is in process.

SECTION FOUR

ANALYZING THE PROBLEM

STEP FOUR ANALYZING THE PROBLEM

IDENTIFY & VERIFY ROOT CAUSES

Most problems usually have multiple and intermingled causes. These causes can usually be classified as root causes or contributory causes.

Identifying each type of cause and then investigating each is necessary to determine which ones actually created the issues of concern.

In following the investigative guidelines it is a good idea adhere closely to the methods applied. This critical phase of the process is the identity of the root cause and must be done with intense care.

One exercise that lends itself to this process is the 5W2H process. (See next page).

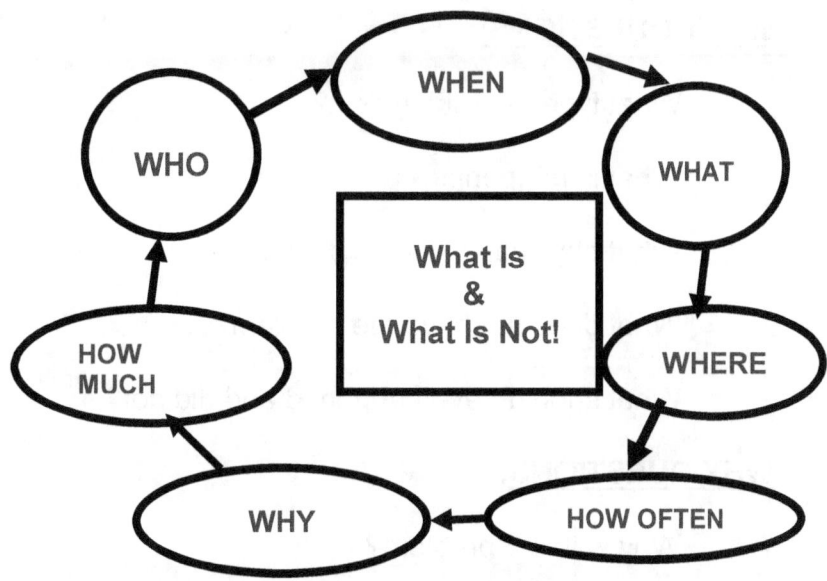

FIGURE #7 5W2H DIAGRAM.

In applying this approach the team will explore what has happened by asking questions as indicated in this diagram and described in the samples beginning on the next page.

WHAT QUESTIONS:

What type of problem is it?

What is happening?

What physical evidence do we have?

What does not have the problem?

What should have happened and did not?

WHY QUESTIONS:

Why is this a problem?

Why is this not a problem?

Why is the process involved stable or unstable?

WHERE QUESTIONS:

Where was the problem observed?

Where wasn't it observed?

Where could it have been observed?

Where did the problem occur?

Where did it not occur?

WHEN QUESTIONS:

When was the problem first noticed?

When has it been noticed since?

When might the problem have been noticed, but was not?

WHO QUESTIONS

Who discovered the Issue?

Who did not observe the Issue?

Who reported the issue?

HOW MUCH (QUANTITY QUESTIONS):

How much is the problem costing in money, time or Manpower?

How may processes could have the problem, but don't?

How big could the problem be, but is not?

HOW OFTEN (FREGUENCY) ?

Trend questions (continuous, random, cyclical)?

What could be the trend but is not?

IDENTIFY CRITICAL ISSUES

For each of the critical issues identified and labeled as a root cause, the Team will be expected to develop potential actions that are likely to correct the issue(s).

One approach to establishing root cause critical issues to a problem is to utilize an Ishakawa or "Fishbone" diagram of cause and effect. This is an excellent tool to guide the brainstorming process needed for the Team to uncover the root causes leading to the issues of nonconformance.

A fishbone diagram for this process is pictured below:

HOW WAS THE ISSUE CREATED?

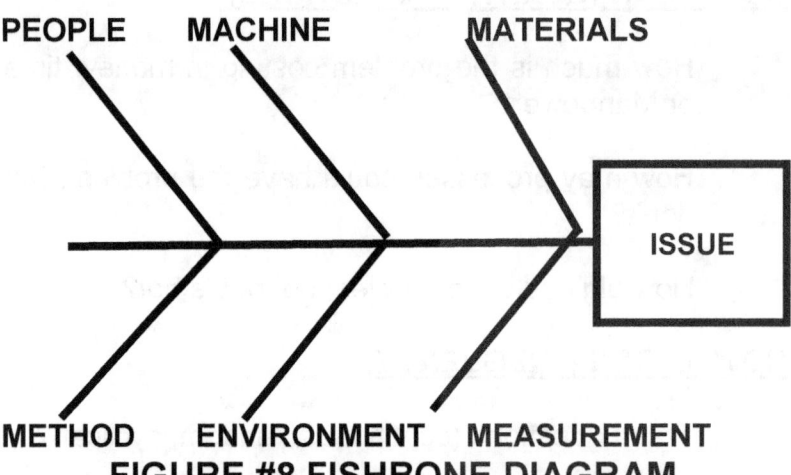

FIGURE #8 FISHBONE DIAGRAM

Questions to be asked for each leg might include the following; however, based upon the issues involved and your specific operations other questions may be more appropriate.

72

PEOPLE LEG:

Who was operating the process?

Were they trained in the process steps?

Were the steps carried out according to instructions given?

MACHINE LEG:

Was the machine operated per instructions?

Had all required preventive and predictive maintenance actions been carried out as required?

MATERIALS LEG:

Was there a change in the materials used in the process?

Is the Material used within approved shelf life dates?

Was proper information provided at the work station?

METHODS LEG:

Were process instructions at the work station clear and appropriate?

Were the instructions current?

Was the process carried out as designed?

ENVIRONMENT LEG:

Were there any changes to the work area environment?

Were there any changes to the material storage environment before or after processing?

MEASUREMENT LEG:

Was the product measured per instructions as to timing, methods, and instruments used?

Was the Operator trained in proper measurement techniques?

Were the measurement instruments used with calibration standards?

Were measurement results recorded properly?

This information when investigated should bring the Team closer to determining the root cause or causes of the outstanding issue. It is however, still to be determined how the nonconforming product was allowed to be delivered to the customer or sent to the next process step for additional value adding.

Once again the fishbone diagram can be a useful approach for guiding the investigative process and establishing what broke down within the process to allow the continued utilization of defective product.

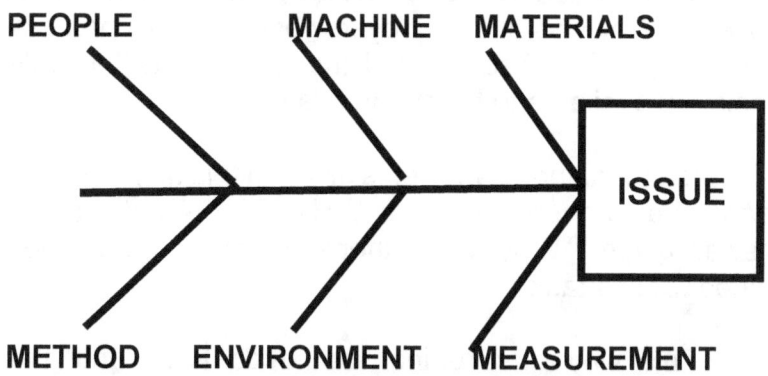

Why did the issue get out?

PEOPLE MACHINE MATERIALS

ISSUE

METHOD ENVIRONMENT MEASUREMENT

FIGURE #9. FISHBONE FOR DETERMINING HOW PRODUCT CONTINUED TO PROCESS AFTER DEFECT WAS CREATED.

In examining each leg of the fishbone, it is suggested that a "Five-Why" approach be used to pursue an answer for what happened to allow the issue to continue processing. In this approach the Team will ask for each leg a "Why" question.
For example:

WHY ANALYSIS
ASK-WHY DID THIS HAPPEN?

ASK-WHY DID THIS HAPPEN?

ASK-WHY DID THIS HAPPEN?

ASK-WHY DID THIS HAPPEN?

ASK-WHY DID THIS HAPPEN?

Each time you answer with a meaningful "Why" you should ask the same question of your answer-Why?

Repeat why process until you believe you have reached the deepest root cause.

FIGURE #10 USING 5-WHY APPROACH TO FIND A ROOT CAUSE!

For the "People" leg, the Team might ask in a situation in which an Operator was not trained in a process; "Why was this employee working at this process sequence?" The Team found that, "This was the only employee available to be put on this task."

If a meaningful answer is given to this question, the Team should then pursue a WHY QUESTION to the answer given. "Why were there no other employees trained for this task?"

This why questioning should continue until the Team believes it has exhausted the why questioning and arrived at the deepest meaningful answer to the question.

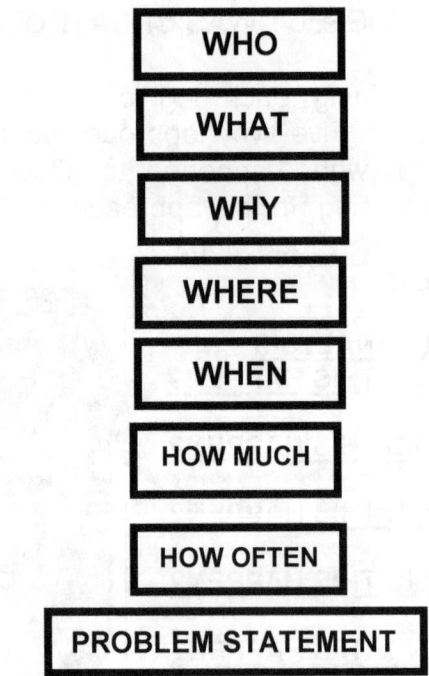

Figure#11...Developing A Root Cause Summary Statement

Once the root cause investigation has been satisfactorily completed, the Team is ready to select the most likely causes to be resolved. This information can then be reduced into a simple problem statement which becomes the focal point for the resolution process.

The next logical step is to utilize the data collected and the problem statement to begin the development of an "Action Plan" for resolving the issues.

SECTION FIVE

CONVERTING ANALYSIS INTO AN ACTION PLAN

IMPLEMENT CORRECTIVE ACTIONS IDENTIFIED:

Based upon the Team's analysis activities, you should now have an accurate listing of process actions that may have led to the issues under investigation. It is now time to lay out a sound plan to resolve the contributing root cause factors, and the resulting issues; thus preventing their recurrence in the future.

A diagram summarizing this process appears below.

ACTION PLAN

USING THE TEAM'S RESULTS FROM BRAINSTORMING, DISCUSSIONS, TND "GEMBA" ACTIVITIES, DEVELOP A ROOT CAUSE ACTION PLAN TO:

VERIFY THE ROOT CAUSES
VALIDATE THE ROOT CAUSES
ESTABLISH A POINT BEYOND WHICH THERE IS NO SUFFICIENT RETURN FROM INVESTIGATION.

DOCUMENT YOUR PROCEDURE AND RESULTS

FIGURE # 12 IDENTIFYING AN ACTION PLAN

This step is critical, as at this stage there needs to be a plan for tracking the resolution process and the corrective action results of what the team has developed. This includes the immediate results as the steps or plan is being implemented. Then a follow-up analysis of results is done after the corrective action has been in place for a while to ensure that the root causes have truly been eliminated.

IDENTIFY SOLUTIONS

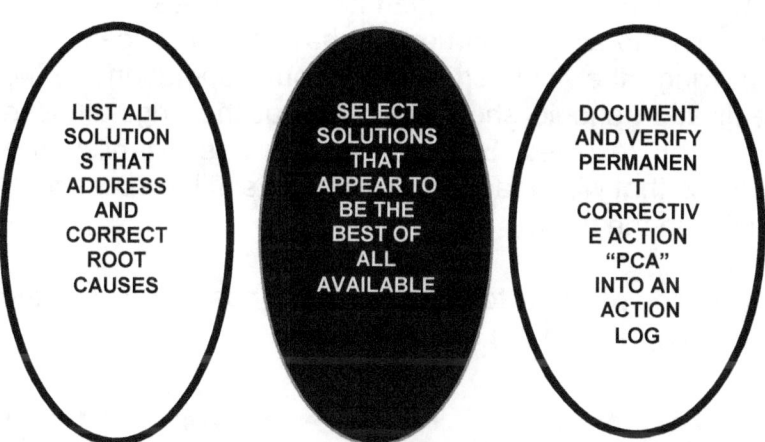

FIGURE #13 IDENTIFYING SOLUTIONS

It is critical that once the root causes for the issue have been clearly and completely identified that they be implemented through a planned implementation process. As each of the corrective actions is carried out all details of the implementation process are to be recorded along with results of the action onto corrective action record table.

SECTION SIX

VALIDATING IMPLEMENTED ACTION PLAN

VALIDATING THE CORRECTIVE ACTIONS TAKEN

Based upon your investigative efforts and within the parameters of the action plan developed to implement corrective actions, the Team should have initiated implementation of actions believed to alleviate the causes which created the problem.

There should therefore be an effort made to verify that the corrective action plan has indeed been effective, and that the actions carried out have been successful in removing the concern from your operations. The verification should show not only that the original issue has been resolved, but that the plan has established a process that will in fact prevent this or similar issues from arising in the future.

The pathway to arrive at such a position is depicted in the diagram on the next page.

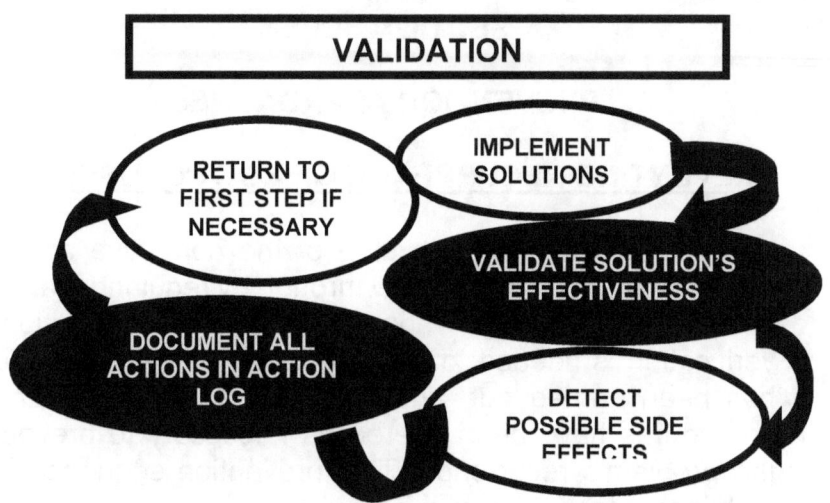

FIGURE #14 SOLUTION VALIDATION DIAGRAM

SECTION SEVEN

PREVENTION APPROACHES

PREVENTING RECURRENCE OF ROOT CAUSES

In this the seventh step of the corrective action process, the Team is to follow through by requiring that all documentary changes be completed. In addition, verification is needed to show that any training required has been carried out, and all operating practices and procedures have been altered as necessary to prevent the problem's recurrence. This prevention sequence is highlighted in the diagram below:

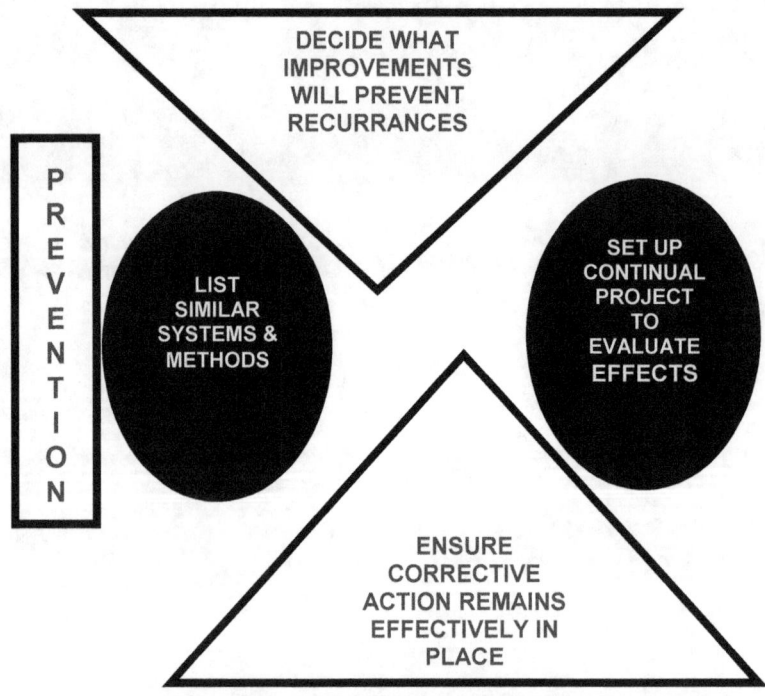

Figure #15...RECURRENCE OF ISSUES AND EXPANDING APPLICATIONS DIAGRAM

In addition to resolving the apparent issue, it is also critical that the Team consider other related applications that might benefit. This process is again primarily one of guided brainstorming by the Team. Below there is a listing depicting some related areas within the makeup of most companies that might readily yield some ideas for benefit expansion.

In the diagram can be seen elements of most operating systems that can be reviewed, discussed, and analyzed to determine how your gains can be shifted to new areas.

POTENTIAL EXTENSION SOURCES

QMS MANUAL
WORK INSTRUCTIONS
IONSPECTION PROCEDURES
FLOW CHARTS
CONTROL PLANS
PROCESS FMEAS
GAUGES/MEASURING DEVICES
PPAPS
ENGINEERING CHANGE APPROVALS
MANUFACTURING FORMS
INSPECTION FORMS
TRAINING PROGRAMS

FIGURE #16 DIAGRAM POSSIBLE SOURCES TO IDENTIFYEXPANDED APPLICATIONS

YEAH TEAM!

TEAM RECOGNITION:

When a problem solving activity has been completed the members should be given recognition for the efforts. Congratulate the team on its success. Whenever possible this recognition should be carried out in such a way that the member's peer groups are aware of their success.

This will make it more likely that others may wish to participate on a problem solving exercise in the future. This recognition need not be financial, but should be supportive and thus encourage additional participation in Problem Solving activities in the future.

MAKE SURE EACH TEAM MEMBER RECEIVES APPROPRIATE RECOGNITION FOR THEIR EFFORTS AND INPUT.

SECTION NINE

APPENDIX "A"

ACTIONS TAKEN TABLE

This form is intended to be a record of the activities carried out during each step of the Eight-D process on a specific issue. The form can then be used as a record of what has been done should such information be needed at a later date.

Another suggestion is that this document be printed in blank form in landscape format, utilizing a heavier weight paper sized (9" X 12"). The form would then be folded in half and used as a file folder to hold a copy of all documentation related to the issue.

See copy of sample form below. The critical thing is not the form of the record however' rather that the critical information listed on the form is retained as the problem solving activity unfolds. These documents could then be pulled for review at a later date, if required.

The form below is just one suggested format. It should be noted that the primary purpose of this form is to record what actions are to be taken, by whom, and by what date or time. In every case we suggest that it be a simple log sheet that you modify to fit your organization.

Corrective Action/Continuous Improvement Record

Issue Title: **Team Leader** **Start Date:**

Note: For each activity row below indicate responsibility assignment/due dates/and verification by entering a date or initials of the individual who completed the action.

Action Needed	Assign To	Due Date	Gemba Action	Fishbone Action	5W2H Action	Five Why Action	Training	Verified
Issue Defined								
Interim Actions								
Root Cause Actions								
Problem Statement								
Possible Solutions								
Actions implemented								
Training Needed								
Actions Verified								
Effectiveness Verified								
Recognition Given								
	Enter Team Member Names/Team Role Title:							
	Note: Comments on Actions Taken/Root Causes Uncovered/Recommended Actions/Training Completed Dates/Corrective Action Verified Dates are to be detailed on back of form. Attach all Pictures							

	Activity Documents or Other Useful Documentation to the Form for Later Reference
	SUMMARIES/COMMENTS/ATTACHMENTS

ACTIVITY COMPLETED	COMMENTS/DETAILS
ISSUE DESCRIPTION	
INTERIM ACTIIONS	
ROOT CAUSE ANALYSIS	
SOLUTIONS CONSIDERED	
CORRECTIVE ACTIONS TAKEN	
TRAINING REQUIRED	
IMPLEMENTATION ACTIIONS	

NEED HELP!

HAVE QUESTIONS OR COMMENTS?

Contact the Author: George "Bill" Browning at:

The Polarity Group
603 Nordic Ct.
Libertyville, IL. 60048
(847) 362-7152
POLARITY GROUP.COM

OTHER POLARITY GROUP PRODUCTS AND SERVICES

OTHER PRODUCTS AVAILABLE

FIVE-S PLUS ADMINISTRATOR'S COMPANION
FIVE-S PLUS LEADER'S GUIDE
FIVE-S PLUS PARTICIPANT'S MANUAL
FIVE-S PLUS SYSTEM POWERPOINT
SEVEN-S PROGRAM FOR PROCESS CONTROL
8-D PROBLEM SOLVING MANUAL
EIGHT-D PROBLEM SOLVING POWERPOINT
POLARITY PROFILE DEVELOPMENT
(MANAGEMENT SKILLS ANALYSIS)

ON-SITE TRAINING SERVICES AVAILABLE

ISO INTERNAL AUDITOR TRAINING
TS-16949 AUDITOR TRAINING
FIVE-S PLUS TRAINING PROGRAM
SEVEN-S PLUS TRAINING PROGRAM
EIGHT-D PROBLEM SOLVING SYSTEM
CONTIUOUS IMPROVEMENT TRAINING
SUPERVISORY TRAINING

ON-SITE AUDITING SERVICES

ISO INTERNAL AUDITING
TS-16949 INTERNAL AUDITING
QUALITY SYSTEM AUDITING

Contact the Author: George "Bill" Browning at:
The Polarity Group
603 Nordic Ct.
Libertyville, IL. 60048
(847) 362-7152
Polarity Group@aol.com

www.ingramcontent.com/pod-product-compliance
Lightning Source LLC
Chambersburg PA
CBHW060400190526
45169CB00002B/690